slave

The Study Guide

slave

THE STUDY GUIDE

The Hidden Truth about Your Identity in Christ

JOHN MACARTHUR

THOMAS NELSON
Since 1798

NASHVILLE   DALLAS   MEXICO CITY   RIO DE JANEIRO

Published in Nashville, Tennessee, by Thomas Nelson. Thomas Nelson is a registered trademark of Thomas Nelson, Inc.

Published in association with the literary agency of Wolgemuth & Associates, Inc.

Thomas Nelson, Inc., titles may be purchased in bulk for educational, business, fund-raising, or sales promotional use. For information, please e-mail SpecialMarkets@ThomasNelson.com.

Unless otherwise noted, Scripture quotations are taken from the New American Standard Bible.® ©The Lockman Foundation 1960, 1962, 1963, 1968, 1971, 1972, 1973, 1975, 1977, 1995. Used by permission.

Scriptures marked NKJV are taken from the New King James Version. © 1982 by Thomas Nelson, Inc. Used by permission. All rights reserved.

ISBN 978-1-4002-0291-1

Printed in the United States of America

10 11 12 13 14 RRD 6 5 4 3 2 1

Contents

One Hidden Word

The young man said nothing else as he stood before the Roman governor, his life hanging in the balance. His accusers pressed him again, hoping to trip him up or force him to recant. But once more he answered with the same short phrase. "I am a Christian" (p. 7).

Rewind

The early martyrs were crystal clear on what it meant to be a Christian. But ask what it means today and you're likely to get a wide of variety of answers, even from those who identify themselves with the label.

For some, being "Christian" is primarily cultural and traditional, a nominal title inherited from a previous generation, the net effect of which involves avoiding certain behaviors and occasionally attending church. For others, being a Christian is largely political, a quest to defend moral values in the public square, or perhaps to preserve those values by withdrawing from the public square altogether. Still more define their Christian experience in terms of a past religious experience, a general belief in Jesus, or a desire to be a good person. Yet all of these fall woefully short of what it truly means to be a Christian from a biblical perspective (p. 10).

What do people around you think the word Christian means?

Based on John 10:27, how do Jesus' expectations of His followers compare with the world's understanding of "Christian"?

Rethink

In addition to the name *Christian*, the Bible uses a host of other terms to identify the followers of Jesus. Scripture describes us as children of God, citizens of heaven, and lights to the world. We are heirs of God and joint heirs with Christ, members of His body, sheep in His flock, ambassadors in His service, and friends around His table. We are called to compete like athletes, to fight like soldiers, to abide like branches in a vine, and even to desire His Word as newborn babies long for milk. All of these descriptions—each in its own unique way—help us understand what it means to be a Christian.

Yet, the Bible uses one metaphor more frequently than any of these. It is a word picture you might not expect, but it is absolutely critical for understanding what it means to follow Jesus. It is the image of a *slave* (p. 12).

What are some characteristics you normally associate with the term *slave*?

How do these characteristics compare to the concept of "Christian" mentioned in question 1?

Early believers knew that following Christ was synonymous with being a slave. Why is the concept of slavery offensive to some believers today?

Many contemporary Christians act as though Jesus came to fulfill their ambitions and make their dreams come true. But that egocentric attitude is at odds with the true gospel. Biblical Christianity is all about Christ. With that in mind, where are you on the continuum below?

It's all about me. $\longleftrightarrow$ It's all about Jesus.

Where would you like to be, and what changes do you need to make to get there?

In the Bible, the word *slave* is almost invisible. Yet it permeates
the pages of Scripture, masquerading as *servant*. For many
people, the term *slave* is offensive, and understandably so. Yet
the Bible clearly teaches that we were purchased by God—we
are His possession. What are the implications of that truth for
our daily lives?

Reflect

True Christianity is not about adding Jesus to *my* life. Instead, it is about
devoting myself completely to *Him*—submitting wholly to His will and
seeking to please Him above all else. It demands dying to self and following
the Master, no matter the cost. In other words, to be a Christian is to be
Christ's *slave* (p. 22).

When Christ says, "Follow Me," what level of commitment is
He calling for? What priority should He be in our lives?

How can we guard against viewing our relationship with
Christ as just something else on our schedules?

How do you determine your priorities each day? What practical steps can you take to ensure that the Lord is central in your daily routine?

Does your day automatically include time for God, or is your time with God optional? Explain your reasoning.

React

Our world tends to view faith as a hobby or a social activity. Today many churches shy away from holding people accountable for the commitments they made when they first accepted Christ. Too many churchgoers are more concerned about getting a good parking spot, having child care, and finding a comfortable place to worship than they are about serving God with their lives. The result is churches that are spiritually weak.

When you go to church, what are your primary concerns? Are they more about you or about God?

What does your attitude at church say about your understanding of what it means to be a slave to Christ? How about your attitude at home or at work?

What are some activities, interests, or passions to which you might be considered a slave? How should you view those things in light of your slavery to Christ?

Where does your relationship with Christ rank in your list of priorities?

__ Absolutely first.

__ Somewhere between _____ and

_____.

__ God gets my leftover time.

two

Ancient History, Timeless Truth

S lavery was a pervasive social structure in the first-century Roman Empire. In fact, it was so commonplace that its existence as an institution was never seriously questioned by anyone. Slaves of all ages, genders, and ethnicities constituted an important socioeconomic class in ancient Rome. Roughly one-fifth of the empire's population were slaves—totaling as many as twelve million at the outset of the first century AD. Not surprisingly, the entire Roman economy was highly dependent on this sizable pool of both skilled and unskilled labor (p. 25).

Rewind

Slavery offered a certain amount of social and economic protection to those whose masters were kind and well respected. Slaves did not have to worry about where their next meal would come from or whether or not they would have a place to stay. Their sole concern was to carry out the interests of their owner. In return, the master cared for their needs. Moreover, if a master was a prestigious or powerful member of the community, such as a government official, his slaves would also be respected because of their relationship to him. A great deal of honor would be given to the slaves of someone highly regarded by Roman society (p. 27).

In reading the description of what it meant to be a slave, what do you consider to be the benefits of slavery for the slave?

A slave's experience depended upon the goodness of his or her master. Since God is our master, what kind of experience should we expect as His slaves?

Rethink

Slavery in the Roman world was as diverse as the number of masters who owned slaves. Whether slaves worked in the fields or in the city; whether they became farmers, household managers, or something else; whether or not they eventually gained their freedom; and whether the quality of their daily existence was positive or negative—everything rested in the hands of the master. Each slave owner defined the nature of his slaves' lives. For their part, slaves had only one primary objective: to please the master in everything through their loyal obedience to him (pp. 28–29).

A slave's objective was to please his master in everything he did. Therefore, as slaves to God, we are to please Him in everything we do. What are some areas of your life in which you are not pleasing the Lord as you should?

The conditions under which slaves worked were often affected by their attitude. A hardworking, submissive slave would be rewarded; an obstinate, grumbling slave would be punished. Describe a time when you have reluctantly done what you knew God wanted you to do.

How would the end result of that situation have been different if your attitude had been more positive?

The exodus from Egypt did not give the Israelites complete autonomy. Rather, it issued them into a different kind of bondage. Those who had once been the property of Pharaoh became the Lord's possession. Read Exodus 19:1–8. How would you have responded if you had been there at the foot of Mount Sinai?

From the Exodus through the Exile and beyond, Israel's corporate identity as God's slaves was an integral part of the nation's history. Many of Israel's heroes, including Abraham, Moses, Joshua, David, Elijah, and the prophets are specifically referred to as His slaves. How does that fact affect your understanding of what it means to be a slave of God?

To be a slave is to be under the complete authority of someone else. It means rejecting personal autonomy and embracing the will of another. Explain why this concept is so offensive to those who live in a society like ours. In what ways does the slave metaphor emphasize the countercultural nature of the gospel?

Reflect

When the apostle Paul referred to himself as a "slave of Christ" and a "slave of God," his readers knew exactly what he meant. In the cities to which Paul wrote, personal freedom was prized, slavery was denigrated, and self-imposed slavery was scorned and despised. But for Paul, "slave" was a fitting self-designation. His life revolved around the Master. Nothing else—including his own personal agenda—mattered.

Prior to his conversion, Paul (then called "Saul") had arrogantly and hypocritically viewed himself as religiously superior to others. What happened that allowed him to view himself as a slave? See Acts 9 for the account of his conversion.

Describe your conversion experience. How did God change your heart, purpose, and priorities?

Read James 1:1. Even though he could have referred to himself first as Jesus' brother, James chose to call himself a slave. What does this say about his perspective on the Christian life?

Read James 4:13–15. How does this passage fit within the slave metaphor? In what ways does it describe the attitude of genuine believers?

How does your attitude toward life compare to that of James?

React

When we survey the New Testament, we quickly find that the term "slave of Christ" was not reserved for low-level believers or spiritual neophytes. The apostles eagerly embraced the title for themselves and also used it to refer to others in ministry. It is not surprising, then, to find slave imagery used frequently throughout their epistles in reference to the Christian life (p. 37).

Our present and future relationships with God are set in the context of slavery. We are to be His slaves now and we will be His slaves in heaven (see Revelation 22:3–4). What should our response to be our God-given role as His slaves?

It's easy for us to see the first Christians as spiritual giants. Yet, they saw themselves as slaves. What effect did that have on their lives? What would happen to the vitality of your Christian life if you embraced the idea of being a slave to Christ?

A slave had no right to his life. He was at the complete mercy of his master. Is the idea of being at God's mercy comforting or frightening to you? Why?

For the slave, there was no area of life outside the boundaries of the master's control. In what areas of life do you need to fully submit to God's control? What would happen if you did that?

Write a prayer asking God to help you become a slave to Him in every area of life.

three

The Good and Faithful Slave

The truth of God's Word is always countercultural, and the notion of becoming a slave is certainly no exception. In fact, it is difficult to imagine a concept more distasteful to modern sensibilities than that of slavery. Western society, in particular, places a high premium on personal liberty and freedom of choice. So, to present the good news in terms of a slave/master relationship runs contrary to everything our culture holds dear. Such an approach is controversial, confrontational, and politically incorrect. Yet that is precisely the way the Bible speaks about what it means to follow Christ (p. 41).

Rewind

Jesus used slave language to define the reality of what it means to follow Him. Discipleship, like slavery, entails a life of total self-denial, a humble disposition toward others, a wholehearted devotion to the Master alone, a willingness to obey His commands in everything, an eagerness to serve Him even in His absence, and a motivation that comes from knowing He is well pleased. Though they were once the slaves of sin, Christ's followers receive spiritual freedom and rest for their souls through their saving relationship with Him (p. 43).

What does it mean to go from being a slave to sin to being a slave to Jesus Christ? How is your life different because of that transformation?

If Jesus, our heavenly Master, were to evaluate your life right now, how pleased would He be with your attitude toward loving God and loving other people?

___ not pleased at all
___ sometimes pleased
___ pleased more often than not
___ always pleased

Rethink

Throughout the New Testament, believers are repeatedly called to embrace the perspective of those who belong to Christ and therefore lovingly submit to Him as Master. That kind of perspective has serious implications for how we, as believers, think and act (pp. 43–44).

Read Romans 6:17–18 and the discussion of *Exclusive Ownership* on pages 44–45. What is the difference between being a slave to Christ and being an employee of Christ? Why is that distinction important?

Read 1 John 2:3. Heartfelt obedience to Christ is evidence that we have come to know Him. Based on your own obedience to the Lord, can you say with confidence that you have come to know Him? Why or why not?

Slaves had only one primary concern, to carry out the will of the master. In areas where they were given direct commands, they were required to obey. In areas where no direct command was given, they were to find ways to please the master as best they could. Read Colossians 3:17, 23. What elements of your life fall outside the boundaries of these verses?

As believers, we can focus on the things God has called us to do, trusting Him to meet our needs. Read Matthew 6:31–33. What are some things that cause you to worry?

Read Philippians 4:6. What should be your attitude regarding the aspects of life mentioned above?

Reflect

In everything they did, first-century slaves were entirely accountable to their owners. Ultimately, the master's evaluation was the only one that mattered. If the master was pleased, the slave would benefit accordingly. A lifetime of faithfulness might even be rewarded with eventual freedom. But if the master was displeased, the slave could expect appropriate discipline, often as severe as flogging (p. 51).

Read Romans 14:12 and 2 Corinthians 5:10. How do these verses make you feel? In what ways should they motivate us toward greater faithfulness? In what ways do they make us thankful for God's loving forgiveness (see 1 John 4:15–18)?

In serving our earthly masters, we also serve the Lord. What should be a believer's attitude at work?

According to Colossians 4:1, Christian masters were to reflect godliness in their attitudes and actions toward slaves. By extension, that same principle applies to all who are in authority over others (such as employers, managers, leaders, and parents). What are some things you can do to better reflect Christ to those under your supervision?

React

Remembering the Master in heaven was a powerful force for the earliest Christians—whether slave or free. It should motivate us as well. Whether or not our faithfulness is rewarded in this life doesn't really matter. One day we will stand before Christ to be recompensed in full (p. 52).

Are you living more for earthly rewards or eternal rewards? Why?

It is easy to live for the praise and adoration of others. What happens to your spiritual fervor when you focus on being accepted by people?

Many believers resist the idea of accountability. They prefer a version of faith that suits their lifestyles and their interests. Many believers attend churches, expecting to receive VIP treatment. How would you evaluate these kinds of attitudes and behaviors in light of the slave mentality presented in the New Testament?

four

The Lord and Master (Part 1)

To this point, we have considered the biblical metaphor of slavery to Christ from the standpoint of the slave, focusing on the word *doulos* and its implications for the Christian life. In this chapter, we will turn our attention to the other side of the slave/master relationship—seeking to understand what the Bible means when it calls Jesus Christ our "Lord" and "Master" (or *kyrios* in Greek). We will begin by considering the truth that He is the Lord and Master over His church (p. 57).

Rewind

John Huss was put to death because he taught that Jesus Christ alone is head of the church. Such statements were offensive to the leaders of the religious establishment of Huss's day. Though they had access to the written Word of God, they chose tradition over obedience. The same decision is being made by many religious leaders today.

> What traditions was John Huss trying to overturn? On what authority did he challenge those traditions?

Why is it important for us to continually evaluate our traditions in light of God's Word? What should we do if our traditions don't measure up to the Scriptures?

Rethink

When John Huss attempted to explain his writings, his voice was drowned out by the angry shouts of his accusers demanding that his books be burned. Though he appealed to reason, to his conscience, and even to the Word of God, his words went completely unheeded and ignored (p. 58).

What happens in our world when believers speak up for the cause of Christ?

What is some evidence that our culture isn't interested in what the Bible has to say?

Slave

Who are some of the people to whom you regularly listen (from television, radio, or personal relationships)? What is their perspective on God? How does their perspective affect their advice?

John Huss argued against any mere man being regarded as the head of the church. Christ alone is the true head. What can we do today to keep Jesus Christ as the focus of our worship?

Huss stood his ground because he valued God's approval more than acceptance by men. Think back on your past two weeks. Have you been more focused on gaining God's approval or man's approval? Why?

What do you need to change about your life so that your focus is more on God and less on self?

Reflect

Huss said that the authority of the Bible is greater than the authority of the church. This was a radical idea in that day, and it was an idea to which Huss had been introduced by John Wycliffe. A hundred years later, Martin Luther would echo this very same conviction.

Many "authorities" in our culture are popular rather than knowledgeable. How do you know which authorities to listen to? What is our final authority as believers?

Truth is contained in the pages of Scripture. Describe your plan for knowing and applying God's Word to your life.

React

John Huss was willing to take a stand for the true gospel even though it cost him his life. His courage was motivated by a heart fully dedicated to God and captivated by His Word. Though the stakes were high, Huss was more concerned with pleasing the Lord than preserving his own safety.

John Huss proved himself faithful even when he faced severe persecution. How should we, as Christians, respond when we are ridiculed or rejected by unbelievers?

Who are some people you know who are steadfast in their faith and unwilling to compromise in any area of life? What lessons have you learned from observing their example?

If threatened with arrest for your belief in God, what would be your response?

five

The Lord and Master (Part 2)

In the first chapter of Ephesians, Paul explained that God the Father "put all things in subjection under His [Christ's] feet, and gave Him as head over all things to the church, which is His body, the fullness of Him who fills all in all" (vv. 22–23). Other New Testament Scripture speaks of growing "up in all aspects into Him who is the head" (Eph. 4:15) and "holding fast to the head, from whom the entire body . . . grows with a growth which is from God" (Col. 2:19) (p. 71).

Rewind

In spite of the clear teaching of Scripture and the faithful witness of Protestant church history, most of the trends in contemporary evangelicalism actually attack the lordship of Christ over His church. Some of these attacks are blatant and theological. The Free Grace view twists the gospel message, claiming that neither repentance from sin nor submission to Christ has any part in saving faith. By promoting a form of "easy believism," Free Grace advocates openly deny the sinner's need to repent of sin and to confess Jesus as Lord and Master in the biblical sense of total submission. In so doing, they teach a different gospel altogether, which is "really not another" but an obvious attempt "to distort the gospel of Christ" (Gal. 1:7).

In what ways have you seen the gospel of Christ distorted?

How can believers today protect themselves against distorted versions of the gospel?

Read Galatians 1:6–9. What is the danger of believing in a distorted version of the gospel?

Rethink

Today the contemporary evangelical movement has lost its interest in doctrine. The current of mainstream evangelicalism is driven by pragmatic concerns, not theological ones. Church growth gurus worry about what draws a crowd, not about what the Bible says. Because it successfully appeals to unredeemed flesh, prosperity preachers make *man* the master, as if Christ were some sort of genie in a bottle—obliged to grant health, wealth, and happiness to those who send enough money. Even within some conservative circles, pragmatic worldly methods (including crass humor and coarse speech) and almost boundless adaptations of the worst of worldly music are aggressively defended as long as they get visible results. The sad reality is that popularity, not faithfulness to Christ and His Word, has become evangelicalism's new standard of measure and its current brand of no-lordship ideology (p. 74).

When you attend church, are you more interested in a good show or in hearing God's truth even if it steps on your toes? Explain your response.

Some of the messages you hear on television, radio, and on the Internet—even from so-called "Christian" ministers—are contradicted by clear biblical teaching. How can you tell the truth from a lie?

The Lord expresses His rule in His church insofar as the Scripture is preached, explained, applied, and obeyed. Think about your church experience and grade each area using a standard school grading system from A to F:

___ Scripture is preached.
___ Scripture is explained.
___ Scripture is applied.
___ Scripture is obeyed.

In what ways is Christ the head of your life? In what areas are you failing to submit to His authority?

Read 1 Corinthians 7:23 and Romans 6:17–18. In the space below, write a summary of what these passages say about a believer's relationship with God.

Read Romans 14:7–8. What does this passage say about the role of the Master in the life of a believer?

Reflect

When the New Testament writers referred to themselves as "slaves of Christ" they underscored their total submission to the lordship of Jesus Christ. For the apostle Paul, this involved nothing less than a life of daily self-sacrifice, wholly lived for the sake of his Master (p. 80).

Read Philippians 1:21. How would you explain Paul's perspective on life? Why could he say that dying is gain?

Believers are often tempted to compromise, disobey, and draw back from their initial commitment to Christ. How can you maintain a fervent focus on the Lord? What should you do when you fail to obey Him (see 1 John 1:9)?

Read Mark 12:30. What are the implications of that verse for your everyday life?

React

Paul was taken prisoner by Jesus on the Damascus Road. His life was changed forever. Though his personality was unaltered, his purpose for living was redefined. His passion was redirected toward things that matter to God. His boldness became a tool that would win many to faith in Christ.

Slave

Read Colossians 3:17, 23. How can you make obedience to these instructions a reality in your life?

God created you with a specific personality for the purpose of glorifying Him through your life. In what ways are you using your abilities and gifts to bring honor to God?

Jesus is the Master, and we are slaves. How does that truth affect your daily life?

six

Our Lord and Our God

The apostles understood that Jesus Christ, being God in human flesh, is far more than any earthly *kyrios*. He is the Lord over every other lord, and the King over every other king. Put succinctly, He is the "Lord of all" (Acts 10:36), possessing the full weight of divine authority, for "in Him all the fullness of Deity dwells in bodily form . . . and He is the head over all rule and authority" (Col. 2:9–10). He has been "SEATED AT THE RIGHT HAND OF THE POWER OF GOD" (Luke 22:69), and all things have been put "in subjection under His feet" (Eph. 1:22). Of Him, the author of Hebrews wrote, "He is the radiance of His [Father's] glory and the exact representation of His nature, and upholds all things by the word of His power. When He had made purification of sins, He sat down at the right hand of the Majesty on high" (1:3). Jesus Christ is "our great God and Savior" (Titus 2:13), the divine Word made flesh, and the promised Messiah, of whom it was foretold, "His name will be called Wonderful Counselor, Mighty God, Eternal Father, Prince of Peace" (Isa. 9:6). The man born blind was not wrong to worship Him after proclaiming, "Lord, I believe" (John 9:38) (pp. 85–86).

Rewind

The New Testament writers repeatedly emphasized Christ's divine authority and equality with God by ascribing the name *kyrios* to Him. For the believers of the early church, the title *kyrios* not only denoted Christ as their absolute Master but also as God. When we confess Jesus as *Lord*, we similarly acknowledge our duty to both obey Him as King and worship Him as Deity (p. 88).

We have a duty to obey and worship God. Read Romans 12:1–2. What is the relationship between our worship and our obedience?

How does the designation *kyrios* relate to the fact that Jesus Christ is God? Why is it such an important title with regard to both His lordship and His deity?

If you were asked to defend the deity of Christ from the New Testament, how would you do it? In addition to passages like John 1:1; 5:18; 20:28 and many others, how does a proper understanding of *kyrios* contribute to the biblical argument?

Rethink

As those who confess the lordship of Christ, believers are duty bound to obey Him in everything. As slaves to righteousness, believers are "under obligation" (Rom. 8:12; cf. 6:18) to honor God in how they live. Yet, for those who belong to Christ, the motivation to obey is far more profound than mere duty. "If you *love* Me, you will keep My commandments," Jesus told His disciples (John 14:15, emphasis added); and again, "If anyone loves Me, he will keep My Word" (v. 23).

> As slaves we are required to obey Christ in everything. Why is this such as hard thing for many believers to do? What is the proper motivation for our obedience to Him?

> Read John 14:15. Genuine believers are characterized by a deep love for Christ, and that love inevitably manifests itself in obedience. Why is it impossible to say you love God and then disobey Him?

The only right response to Christ's lordship is wholehearted submission, loving obedience, and passionate worship. In your own words, describe how those three concepts are related to one another. Why are they a proper response to Christ's authority?

Read Luke 6:46. What would you say if Jesus asked you this question? Is there any area of your life where that question might apply?

Reflect

Though many call themselves "Christians," the true condition of anyone's heart is ultimately seen in how he lives. As the saying goes, actions speak louder than words. The profession of faith that never evidences itself in righteous behavior is a "dead" faith (James 2:17), being no better than that of the demons (v. 19). This is not to say that true believers never stumble. Certainly they do. Yet the pattern of their lives is one of continual repentance and increasing godliness as they grow in sanctification and Christlikeness (pp. 92–93).

If actions speak louder than words, then what is your lifestyle saying about your love for God?

Are you satisfied with your response to the question above? Why or why not?

What do you need to change in your life so that your actions match what you claim to believe?

React

Because the Lord is our Master, we can trust Him to take care of us in every situation and stage of life. Even in the most difficult of circumstances, He will provide all that we need in order to be faithful to Him (p. 94).

Slave

The life of a slave results in the ultimate experience of peace and joy. Read Philippians 4:6. If your peace and joy are indicators of your level of confidence in God, how well are you doing at trusting Him in all things?

What decisions or challenges are you facing? How can you trust God to see you through those situations?

The greatest glory for a slave is the realization that he is honoring his master. As you pray, ask God to give you the passion for serving Him with joy and sharing the truth about Him with confidence. Write your prayer in the space below.

seven

The Slave Market of Sin

If anyone understood the horrors and abuses of the eighteenth-century slave trade, it was John Newton. He had experienced slavery from both sides—having lived as a slave in Africa and having participated in the trade after returning home. As a minister, he had written about the abuses of slavery, and in the end, he was instrumental in bringing the British slave trade to its end. Christians today can rejoice in God's providential use of John Newton—not only by saving him personally from his wicked past but also by using him (along with William Wilberforce and others) to end one of modern history's great injustices (p. 110).

Rewind

Newton's unique testimony gave him a deep sense of appreciation for God's rescuing mercy in his life. His past experiences helped him understand what it truly meant to be a *slave of sin*—to be hopelessly oppressed and exploited by a wicked master. He often reflected on the harsh reality of his own enslavement, drawing parallels from his experience to the spiritual reality of sin's bondage (p. 110–11).

In what ways does the uniqueness of your testimony help you realize what it means to be a slave to sin?

As a believer in Jesus Christ, how does it make you feel to recognize that you have been set free from sin?

Rethink

John Newton repeatedly contrasted bondage to sin with the redemption he received through Jesus Christ. He portrayed himself in his lost condition as a slave who, if Christ had not rescued him, would have remained in captivity. Newton's hymns resound with the glorious theme of deliverance from his own wickedness. Newton remembered what it was like to be unconverted, to be one of those who was under Satan's complete control.

Compare your bondage to sin to the redemption you received at salvation. How can you describe the difference between these two states of existence?

If your life were declared in a hymn, what would be its theme? Why do you think Newton's hymn "Amazing Grace" has resounded with so many people?

The reality is that we are never free; our lives are always under the control of something or someone. As unbelievers, we lived under the power of sin. But now we are under the power of God. What differences have you seen in your life as a result of that radical change?

Read Romans 8:1. As believers, we have not only been set free from sin's oppression but also from its deadly consequences. How does that make you feel, as you consider the difference between the wages of sin and the free gift of eternal life?

Reflect

Newton understood the ethical implications of his freedom in Christ. Though he had been rescued from the evil oppression of sin, he now had a new Master, the Lord Jesus Christ. But unlike sin—the most wicked and cruel of all oppressors—Christ is the perfect Master, being righteous, just, gracious, and good. To submit to His will is pure joy.

If submission to God's will is pure joy, why do so many believers resist obeying God's will for their lives?

What are some of the ethical implications of your freedom in Christ?

Read Ephesians 5:3–10. How should believers respond to those who, under the guise of friendship, will have a negative influence on them?

How do you guard your moral purity in a world that seems to have no moral standards?

What are some things you have eliminated from your life in order to protect yourself from immoral and unethical influences?

React

John Newton compared the Christian's deliverance from sin to Israel's deliverance from Egypt. Like Pharaoh, sin is the harshest of taskmasters. Christians, like the Israelites, can rejoice in being rescued by God's grace.

In what way is Israel's physical liberation from Egypt a picture of the spiritual liberation that sinners experience when they are set free from sin?

Read Romans 6:23. Do you agree that sin is a harsh taskmaster? Why or why not?

Once rescued from slavery, the Israelites returned to the bondage of disobedience. How does your knowledge of God's Word protect you from the bondage of disobedience?

eight

Bound, Blind, and Dead

Early Christians would have been well aware of the abuses a slave could suffer at the hands of an unjust owner. Many first-century believers were slaves themselves, and some of them were subjected to harsh and unfair treatment. Peter instructed believers saying, "Be submissive to your masters with all respect, not only to those who are good and gentle, but also to those who are unreasonable. For this finds favor, if for the sake of conscience toward God a person bears up under sorrows when suffering unjustly" (1 Peter 2:18–19) (p. 119).

Rewind

It is against a cultural backdrop replete with the knowledge and acceptance of slavery that the New Testament speaks of slavery to sin and of sin's reign in the human heart. Sin is the vilest, most dreadful master imaginable— a reality which would not have been lost on first-century believers. They would have naturally drawn parallels from the worst abuses in their culture, understanding the total subjugation that such slavery entailed.

> Read 1 Peter 2:18–19. How were the physical slaves in the early church instructed to respond to their earthly masters?

How would a harsh master have served as an illustration of the oppression that characterizes sin?

Roman slaves were at the mercy of their masters. Before salvation, we were also at the mercy of a master—sin. How has your life changed since being freed from slavery to sin?

As believers, we are now slaves to God. He is the most wonderful Master imaginable. Why is slavery to God a liberating reality? How is it different from slavery to sin?

Rethink

Sin corrupts the entire person—infecting the soul, polluting the mind, defiling the conscience, contaminating the affections, and poisoning the will. It is the life-destroying, soul-condemning cancer that festers and grows like an incurable gangrene in every unredeemed human heart.

We have a tendency in our culture to minimize sin—making light of its effects. By contrast, how does God's Word describe the seriousness of sin?

Read John 8:34. Jesus was explaining that unbelievers are enslaved by their sin. Now read verse 36. What is the sinner's only hope of freedom from sin? Look again at verses 31–32. How does Jesus define true freedom?

How does Jesus' description of freedom in John 8:31–32 fit with your own understanding of freedom? In what ways does your understanding of freedom need to change?

"Scripture is clear: unless the Spirit of God gives spiritual life, all sinners are completely unable to change their fallen nature or to rescue themselves from sin and divine judgment. They can neither initiate nor accomplish any aspect of their redemption" (p. 122). In light of passages such as Ephesians 2:1–10, do you agree with this statement? Why or why not?

Pride makes us think we are not as sinful as we really are. We rationalize our sin by focusing on the more significant sins of others. Read Luke 18:10–14. What is God's response to prideful, self-righteous people?

Reflect

The Bible teaches that unbelievers wholeheartedly love their sin. They are not only utterly *unable* to free themselves from its corruption; they are also obstinately *unwilling* to do so. As Jesus told the religious leaders of His day, "You search the Scriptures because you think that in them you have eternal life; it is these that testify about Me; and you are *unwilling* to come to Me so that you may have life" (John 5:39–40, emphasis added) (p. 124).

Jesus spoke to people who were involved in religious activity, yet they hypocritically clung to sin in their hearts. What they claimed to believe contradicted the way they lived. What is the relationship between what you claim to believe and the way you live?

Read Romans 3:10–12. In light of Paul's words, how can you and I (or any sinner) stand blameless before God?

"Left to his own natural reason and volition, the unredeemed sinner will always choose slavery to sin over obedience to God. Until the Lord intervenes, the sinner is neither able nor willing to abandon his sin and serve God in righteousness" (p. 126). Read Romans 6:1–2. If someone claims to be a believer yet continues to live like a slave to sin, what is that person's true attitude toward God's grace?

When we become believers, sin's power over our lives is broken. Yet we still struggle in our battle against our sinful flesh, needing to continually confess our sins and repent from them (1 John 1:9). In your fight against sin, what are three areas in which you face repeated temptation?

What is your strategy for resisting these temptations? To whom should you be accountable so you can guard yourself in these areas?

React

Apart from divine intervention, the slave of sin remains in an utterly helpless and hopeless situation. He is not only powerless to free himself, but he wears his chains with willing eagerness (p. 127).

In the space below, list some people you know who, as unbelievers, openly flaunt their slavery to sin.

In every relationship, you are either the influencer or you are being influenced. In regard to the people mentioned above, are you having a positive spiritual impact on them, or are they leading you into a lifestyle you claim to have abandoned?

In what specific ways can you pray for the people you listed? Only the truth of the gospel can set them free from their sin. Will you commit yourself to sharing the good news of salvation with these people?

nine

Saved from Sin, Slaved by Grace

It is from slavery to sin that God saves His elect, rescuing them from the domain of darkness and transferring them as His own slaves into the kingdom of His Son (Col. 1:13). When we loved nothing but ourselves and our sin, God first loved us, such that we might respond to Him in faith. As the apostle John explains, "In this is love, not that we loved God, but that He loved us and sent His Son to be the propitiation for our sins.... We love Him because He first loved us" (1 John 4:10, 19 NKJV). In saving us from slavery to sin, God initiated and accomplished everything. Were it not for His purposeful intervention, we would still be helplessly in bondage to sin (p. 131).

Rewind

As those chosen by God, believers were predestined to be freed from slavery to sin and ushered into the household of God. He pursued us even though we did not seek Him, drawing us to Himself and snatching us from the clutches and condemnation of sin. Like Paul, we were "laid hold of by Christ Jesus" (Phil. 3:12), becoming His willing captives, His joyful prisoners, and part of the people for His own possession. We are those who belong to Him, not because we chose Him but because He chose us (pp. 132–33).

How does it make you feel knowing that God chose you even though you did not deserve it?

If God predestined us to be freed from slavery to sin, why do so many professing Christians remain entangled in sinful lifestyles? Read 1 John 2:4–5. How valid is a profession of faith that does not result in a transformed life?

Rethink

"God's will in salvation is singular, dependent on nothing other than His uninfluenced, free, electing choice. Therefore, the Holy Spirit works where He wills, the Son gives life to whomever He wishes, and unless the Father draws them, unbelievers cannot come to Christ" (p. 134). Read the following Scriptures and briefly summarize each:

John 8:36
2 Corinthians 4:6
Ephesians 2:4–5

God's sovereign grace includes not only the gift of salvation but also the repentant faith necessary for receiving that gift. In light of that, how much of our salvation can we take credit for? What should our response be to God for initiating and accomplishing everything in our salvation?

Read 2 Thessalonians 2:13–14. What does this passage say about you and God's purpose for your life?

The only reason we could respond in love to God was because He first loved us. Read John 3:16. How can you help nonbelieving friends understand the magnitude of God's love?

Reflect

Our redemption in Christ results in both *freedom* from sin and *forgiveness* for sin. Not only are we liberated from bondage to our former master; we are also exempt from sin's deadly consequences—namely, the eternal wrath of God. As Paul exclaimed in Romans 8:1–2, "Therefore there is now no condemnation for those who are in Christ Jesus. For the law of the Spirit of life in Christ Jesus has set you free from the law of sin and of death." Because we are in Him, all of our sins—past, present, and future—have been "forgiven [us] for His name's sake" (1 John 2:12) (p. 139).

Read Romans 8:1–2. Which law is controlling your life? How do you know?

God's gift of redemption brings salvation from both sin's oppression and sin's consequences—and one day from its very existence. Though we are freed from the eternal consequences of sin, we are still subject to the earthly consequences of our sin. Think about your life and the temptations you face. If you were to give in to those temptations, what might some of the earthly consequences be?

Slave

In what way is the fear of such consequences a deterrent to sin?

Fill in the blanks with either *Christ* or *sin*: Unlike _____, _____ is the perfect Master. _____ is the cruelest and most unjust of all masters; _____ is the most loving and merciful. _____'s burden is heavy and loathsome; _____'s yoke is easy and the burden is light. _____ traps its slaves in darkness and death; _____ brings light and life to all those who have been made alive. _____ diverts, deceives, and destroys; _____ is the way, the truth, and the life. Insofar as slavery to _____ consists of everything hateful, harmful, dreadful, and despicable, so slavery to _____ entails everything good, glorious, joyous, and right.

Based on your life, are you enslaved to Christ or to sin?

What would your friends or family say about you in response to the question above?

Read Romans 6:23. What are the wages of sin? What is the gift that comes through faith in Christ? Which offers the better result? Why?

React

True freedom begins when slavery to sin ends, and slavery to sin ends only when we have become the slaves of God.

The freed in Christ are not aimless or purposeless. They have been freed from sin in order that they may give themselves wholly to serving God. How are you serving God—with your time, energy, talents, and money?

To invest your life in a way that pleases God, what activities do you need to adjust or eliminate?

Our freedom in Christ does not give us the right to decide what is right or wrong. We are obligated to pursue righteousness and right living, as delineated for us in the Word of God. What are some biblical boundaries you need to establish or reinforce in your own life?

From Slaves to Sons (Part 1)

When God rescues unbelievers from sin, He makes them His own slaves. Yet, He does not stop there. In salvation, the redeemed become not only His slaves but also His friends (John 15:14–15), as well as citizens in His kingdom and, most notably, adopted children in His family. Believers have been transformed from slaves of sin into the sons and daughters of righteousness (pp. 148–49).

Rewind

Fourth-century church father John Chrysostom said many centuries ago:

> First there is the freeing from sin, and then there is the making of slaves of righteousness, which is better than any freedom. For God has done the same as if a person was to take an orphan who had been carried away by savages into their own country, and was not only to free him from captivity but to set a kind of father over him and raise him to a very great dignity. This is what has happened in our case. For it was not just that God freed us from our old evils; He also led us into the life of angels. He opened the way for us to enjoy the best life, handing us over to the safekeeping of righteousness and killing our former evils, putting the old man in us to death and bringing us to eternal life. (p. 149)

Think about your life and describe how you have experienced each of the following:

+ Being set free from sin's control:

+ Becoming a slave to righteousness:

+ Realizing that you are a child of God:

Our salvation experience puts the old man to death and brings new life. Would your friends say you exhibit more evidence of the old man or the new life? Why?

Rethink

Having delivered us from the destitution of sin, God not only receives us as His slaves—but He has also welcomed us into His household and made us members of His very family. He not only rescued us, purchased us, befriended us, and took us in; He has also adopted us, thereby transforming those who were formerly children of wrath (Ephesians. 2:3) into the sons and daughters of righteousness (p. 155).

We have been adopted into God's family. Why is human adoption such a powerful metaphor of this spiritual reality? What thoughts come to mind as you consider God's love toward us?

Read Romans 8:14–17. Explain these verses in your own words.

As the adopted children of God, we can rest assured in knowing that we have been given a permanent place in the family of God. What is your attitude toward God in response to that biblical truth?

Read Ephesians 5:8 and Hebrews 12:7. In light of the fact that we are God's children and He is our Father, how should we conduct ourselves in this world?

Reflect

Unlike earthly fathers, who are sometimes prone to anger and harshness, God is a perfect Father. Moreover, because of our position in Christ, God now views us and treats us as He does His own Son—with infinite love. The Father cannot give anything but His best to His Son. Likewise, He will not give anything but His best to those of us who are in Christ (pp. 157–58).

Read Romans 8:28. What does this verse say? Note that this verse does not promise that God will fulfill our every wish but, rather, that He will orchestrate every situation for our spiritual good. How does that promise fit with James 1:2–4?

Read Galatians 4:4–7. There Paul explains that we are no longer slaves to sin since we have been adopted into the family of God. How would you explain this passage to someone who doesn't understand what it means to be a follower of Christ?

Take a moment to read Romans 8. List below three to four main points Paul made in this passage.

How does each of these points affect the way you view your relationship with God?

React

To think that we, who were once the slaves of sin, the subjects of Satan, and the sons of disobedience, are now and forever the slaves of Christ, the citizens of heaven, and the children of God—such is the joy and wonder of salvation. As His enemies, we did not even deserve to be His slaves (cf. Luke 15:19). Yet He has made us both His slaves and His children. The incomparable reality of adoption is this: If God is our Master, then He is also our Father. And vice versa (p. 160).

Read the paragraph above and write down your initial reaction to the truths it contains.

In what ways can you better reflect God's unconditional love toward the people you encounter each day?

If God is our Master, then He is our Father; if He is our Father, then He is also our Master. Explain in your own words how those two realities fit together.

Read Matthew 6:31–34. As a child of God, you can trust your heavenly Father for your needs. What needs are you trusting God to meet in your life right now?

How do you distinguish between needs and wants?

eleven

From Slaves to Sons (Part 2)

Though the process takes months, everything changes for the child when the judge finally declares him to be the legal heir of his adoptive parents. Had the child been left in the orphanage or in the care of abusive and neglectful birth parents, the outcome would likely have been tragic. But now, through the intervention of those who were formerly strangers, a little boy or girl is given a brand-new home filled with the love of a family and the hope of a future. Such is the miracle of adoption.

The New Testament builds on the joy and wonder of human adoption by using it as an analogy to describe God's fatherly love for us. We had no home but this world, no guardian but Satan, and no future but hell. Had we been left in that condition, we would have died in our sins and perished eternally. At great cost to Himself, God intervened to rescue us from sin and bring us into fellowship with Him. In that moment, the Judge of the universe declared us righteous, having clothed us in the sinless perfection of Jesus Christ. He made us His slaves, brought us into His kingdom, and welcomed us into His family. Such is the miracle of our spiritual adoption (pp. 163–64).

Rewind

One of the first adoptions recorded in the Old Testament was that of Moses, whose life was spared when his mother floated him down the Nile

River in a waterproof basket. When Pharaoh's daughter came to the river and found him, she took pity on him. Miriam—Moses' sister, who had been watching from nearby—offered to find a suitable nursemaid for the baby, and Pharaoh's daughter agreed. As a result, Moses was returned to his birth mother until he was old enough to go live in the palace. Thus, Moses—the son of slaves—became part of the royal family of Egypt (pp. 164–65).

Describe how you feel knowing that you were rescued from certain eternal judgment and given new life as the child of the King.

Read 2 Corinthians 6:17–18. What does this passage say about your relationship with God? According to the very next verse, 2 Corinthians 7:1, what are the implications of that relationship?

Rethink

The story of David and Mephibosheth, told on pages 165–66, is a magnificent picture of our spiritual adoption by God. We were not seeking Him, yet, as David found his slain enemy's only remaining heir and took him in, God found *us* and took us in—and saved us. We were His enemies, yet He made us His friends. We could offer Him nothing in return, yet He bestowed on us an inheritance we did not deserve. All of this is ours by grace through faith in His only begotten Son, Jesus Christ.

As adopted slaves, our names are written in the Book of Life, from which they can never be erased. What inheritance is yours because of your status as God's child?

Read 2 Corinthians 4:17–18. In what ways does the reality of your future inheritance change the way you look at the trials of this life? How does the assurance of eternal life affect the way you live each day?

Read Romans 8:15. What was Paul's message to his readers? Why was this message important to them?

Why is this message important today?

Read Ephesians 1:3–6. List some of the spiritual blessings that God has given to believers through Jesus Christ.

Read Psalm 16:5, noting David's emphasis on God being His inheritance. For David, everything was viewed in light of His relationship with the Lord. Do you view life from a God-centered perspective, or do you view God from a world-centered perspective?

What is the difference between these two perspectives?

Reflect

If our adoption were not permanent, we would have great reason to fear. Our sin would condemn us. We did nothing to earn our adoption into God's family, and we can do nothing to lose it either.

Look again at Romans 8:15. Why do we no longer need to be afraid? How does this verse compare to 1 John 4:17–18?

Read Romans 8:29–31. What is the promise to those whom God justifies? What does this promise mean to you today?

Read 1 John 2:19–20. A true believer can never lose his salvation. Once adopted into God's family, he becomes a child of God forever. According to this verse, what is the spiritual condition of one who claims to know Christ but later falls away?

Read John 6:39–40. What did Jesus say about the possibility that a believer could be taken away from Him? How does this passage compare with John 10:28–29?

React

Those who persist in unrepentant sin demonstrate that they have never truly been adopted into God's family, no matter what they profess (1 John 2:4–5). The true children of God inevitably manifest the character traits of their new family. Moreover, having been rescued from sin and adopted by God, their hearts are filled with gratitude and love for the Father who saved them (p. 174).

What do the following passages say about your position as a believer?

Romans 8:1

1 Peter 1:5

Philippians 1:6

1 Thessalonians 5:23–24

2 Thessalonians 3:3

Jude 24–25

Read Romans 6:1. Since we are forgiven, why is it important that believers refrain from sinning?

To continue in a lifestyle of sin after "salvation" is evidence that the person never really experienced salvation (1 John 1:6). How do those who know you best know that your salvation is real?

As God's children, we should no longer fear death, because it will usher us into the presence of our heavenly Father. How has your attitude toward death changed since you accepted Jesus as your Lord and Savior?

twelve

Ready to Meet the Master

In Matthew 25, Jesus painted a word picture for His disciples [using a parable that begins] like this: "[The kingdom of heaven] is just like a man about to go on a journey, who called his own slaves and entrusted his possessions to them. To one he gave five talents, to another, two, and to another, one, each according to his own ability; and he went on his journey. . . . Now after a long time the master of those slaves came and settled accounts with them" (vv. 14–15, 19).

The slaves in Jesus' story are urban slaves—domestic stewards who had been given the responsibility of managing the master's estate in his absence. Yet the situation is similar to that of a rustic slave anticipating his master's arrival. In both cases, the master is away for a prolonged period. While he is gone, he expects the slaves to supervise his estate and further his interests. When he returns, he will inspect their work and either praise or punish them as a result (p. 180).

Rewind

In our Lord's parable, two of the slaves applied themselves diligently to their task. Both of them doubled the amount of money they had received. When the master finally returned, he was exceedingly pleased with the work they had done.

But the third slave squandered his opportunity to invest—having hidden his portion in a hole in the ground. The master's displeasure resounded in words of condemnation. "You wicked, lazy slave, . . . you ought to have put my money in the bank, and on my arrival I would have received my money back with interest. Therefore take away the talent from him, and give it to the one who has the ten talents" (vv. 26–28). While these words were still ringing in his ears, the worthless slave was thrown "into the outer darkness; in that place there will be weeping and gnashing of teeth" (v. 30).

The imagery is clear. The master represents Christ, and his prolonged absence pictures the time between Christ's ascension and His second coming. The slaves are professing believers who have been entrusted, as stewards, with various resources, abilities, blessings, and opportunities. One day, they will all be called to give an account for that stewardship (p. 181).

If called upon today to give an account for your stewardship of the resources, abilities, blessings, and opportunities entrusted to you, what would you say to God?

Based on the parable above, what would God's reaction be to your stewardship?

What are some ways you can do better at investing the resources God has given you for His purposes?

Rethink

Though we do not know when the Master will return, we do know one thing for certain: *one day He will come back* (Mark 13:33–37). That simple fact should motivate us to greater holiness and service. It should also comfort and enthuse us, if we are living obediently. A slave only fears the master's return if he has been unfaithful. But for Christ's slaves who have worked hard and served well, the Master's arrival is a moment of great celebration. For them, His coming represents entrance into His joy and the beginning of great reward (p. 183).

Read Philippians 2:10–11. Every person will make the declaration described in this passage. What is the difference between those who make the declaration while they are alive and those who make the declaration at judgment?

Slave

The obedient slave has nothing to fear in the Master's return. Where are you on the line below?

disobedient/afraid ⟵————————⟶ obedient/unafraid

Where would you like to be on the line above? What needs to change in order for you to be there?

Those believers who spend their lives in temporal and worthless pursuits should expect minimal reward from Christ. Based on your spiritual investment, what degree of reward should you expect from God?

Read Ephesians 6:5–9. Take note of its emphasis on the believer's future evaluation and reward from Christ. What would you say to a new believer who asks, "How should I live my life?"

How consistent is your life with the advice you would offer?

Though he would often be rejected and persecuted, Paul was far more concerned with obeying his divine calling than with gaining man's approval. Only one thing mattered—pleasing the Master. What is your primary concern in life?

How does your commitment to Christ compare to the commitment we see in Paul's life?

Reflect

When Paul was falsely accused, his response was simple and steadfast. When imprisoned and awaiting death, he was the picture of calm confidence. At the close of his life, as he sat alone in a Roman dungeon, Paul could still smile at the future. Words of hope pervaded his perspective because he measured success by a heavenly standard.

By what standard are you measuring success?

If you achieve the American Dream, what will be God's reaction? Read Mark 8:36. How important is worldly wealth when compared to eternity?

How can believers live on earth as citizens of heaven?

Citizenship provides certain privileges. What are some of the privileges of citizenship in heaven?

Citizenship also brings certain responsibilities. What are some of your responsibilities as a citizen of heaven? How effectively are you carrying out your responsibilities? What excuses are you making for not doing what God has called you to do?

React

There is an incredible responsibility that comes with being part of Christ's kingdom. As His subjects, we must properly represent Him. Accordingly, we are commanded to "walk in a manner worthy of the God who calls you into His own kingdom and glory?" (1 Thess. 2:12) (p. 193).

What does it mean to "walk in a manner worthy of the God who calls you into His own kingdom and glory" (1 Thess. 2:12)?

Our life is synonymous with our citizenship. Our priorities, passions, and pursuits have all been changed, because our very identity has been transformed. In what ways have the following been transformed in your life:

+ Priorities?

+ Passions?

+ Pursuits?

Read Revelation 22:3–5. What should be the effect of this passage on your attitude toward life?

Are you living with this expectation? Why or why not?

thirteen

The Riches of the Paradox

While nothing in the Bible is contradictory, many of the Bible's most provocative and profound truths appear to us paradoxical. Consider, for example, the truth that salvation is both free and costly, or that to be truly rich you must be poor in spirit, or that to find your life you must lose it, or that to be wise you must embrace the foolishness of the gospel. Scripture teaches that those who mourn will be comforted; those who give will receive; those who are least will be greatest; those who are humble will be exalted; and those who are last will be first. We learn, further, that God uses evil for good; that He is three yet one; and that Jesus Christ, the second member of the Trinity, is simultaneously fully God and fully man. These are just some of the wondrous mysteries that the Bible sets forth.

To this list, we could certainly add the biblical teaching regarding slavery to Christ. A metaphor commonly associated with scorn, oppression, and abuse, *slavery* has been glorious transformed, in Christ, to signify honor, liberty, and eternal bliss (p. 197)!

Rewind

We have considered the crucial difference between *servants* and *slaves*— noting that while servants are hired, slaves are owned. Believers are not merely Christ's hired servants; they are His slaves, belonging to Him as His possession. He is their Owner and Master, worthy of their unquestioned allegiance and absolute obedience. His Word is their final authority; His will, their ultimate mandate (p. 198).

> The Lord has expressed His will in His Word—giving us the commands and guidelines that we are to follow as His slaves. If we are to be faithful to Him, we must know and submit to His Word. What practical steps can you take to learn and understand God's Word better?

> Would you say that you are living to please yourself or to please God?

> What is the difference between those two vantage points?

In your own words, define what it means to be a slave of Christ. How is that different from merely being His servant?

Rethink

As Christians, *we are slaves of Christ.* What a radical difference that truth should make in our daily lives! We no longer live for ourselves. Rather, we make it our aim to please the Master in everything (p. 202).

As we conclude this study, let's consider the four paradoxes described on pages 200–211.

Slavery Brings Freedom—true freedom can only be found through slavery to Christ. Why is this truth so hard for many modern Christians to accept? Read Romans 6:16–18. What did Paul say about this issue?

Slavery Ends Prejudice—slavery to Christ is the path to reconciliation and unity within the body of Christ. When believers realize that they are all *slaves*, called to model the humility of the ultimate slave, it becomes obvious how they ought to treat others.

Read Philippians 2:5–7. If our attitude should be the same as Christ's, how should we treat other people? Why is it significant that He took on the form of a slave (v. 7)?

Slavery Magnifies Grace—our slavery to Christ magnifies the wonder of His infinite grace. It is important to understand that our service to Him is also an undeserved gift—one we both receive and accomplish by His grace. Our ability to serve Him is only possible because He enables us to do so "by the strength which God supplies; so that in all things God may be glorified through Jesus Christ" (1 Peter 4:11).

Read Matthew 6:24. What are some of the "masters" that deter people from submitting to the one, true Master?

Read 1 Corinthians 15:10 and 2 Corinthians 5:9. What was Paul's attitude toward serving God? What is your attitude toward serving God?

Slavery Pictures Salvation—God has expressed the riches of our salvation using the symbolism of slavery. In eternity past, God chose those whom He would save. In our own lifetimes, He rescued us from slavery to sin and delivered us into the kingdom of His dear Son. Christ's atoning work on the cross redeemed us, such that we were purchased by Him; and having been bought with a price, we are now His possession. We have been liberated from sin, and now as slaves to righteousness, we possess a glorious freedom that will be ours for all of eternity future.

Read Titus 2:11–14. Explain this passage in your own words.

Salvation is by faith alone. Yet genuine saving faith is never alone. It inevitably produces "fruit in keeping with repentance" (Matt. 3:8), thereby evidencing a transformed heart. In what ways has your life been transformed?

Reflect

We end this book where we began—asking the question, *What does it mean to be a Christian?* What is your response?

React

Let's rephrase the question above—How has your study of slavery to Christ impacted your understanding of the Christian life? What are the implications of that concept in your daily walk with God?

What are your closing thoughts in regard to your status as God's slave?

Leader
Guide

One Hidden Word

Read chapter 1 of *Slave* and complete the activities in chapter 1 of the Study Guide.

Rewind

- Write *martyr* on the board and call for volunteers to suggest meanings. List responses on the board.
- Ask, "What do people around you think the word *Christian* means?" Discuss responses.
- Read aloud John 10:27 and ask, "How do Jesus' expectations of His followers compare with the world's understanding of *Christian?*" Discuss responses.

Rethink

- Explain that the Bible uses a host of other terms to identify the followers of Jesus. Scripture describes us as children of God, citizens of heaven, and lights to the world. We are heirs of God and joint heirs with Christ, members of His body, sheep in His flock, ambassadors in His service, and friends around His table. We are called to compete like athletes, to fight like soldiers, to abide like branches in a vine, and even to desire His Word as newborn babies long for milk. All of these descriptions—each in its own unique way—help us understand what it means to be a Christian.

+ Write *slave* on the board and call for learners to suggest some characteristics of slaves. List responses on the board.

+ Ask, "How do these characteristics compare to the concept of Christian discussed earlier?" Discuss responses.

+ Arrange learners in small groups and instruct them to discuss some reasons the concept of slavery is offensive to some believers today. Call for groups to report.

+ Explain that the word *slave* is almost invisible in the Bible. Yet it permeates the pages of Scripture, masquerading as *servant*. For many people, the term *slave* is offensive, and justifiably so. Yet the Bible clearly teaches that we were purchased by God—we are His possession. Ask, "What are the implications of that truth for our daily lives?" Discuss responses.

Reflect

Submission to Christ ought to be our highest priority. It should permeate everything we do. While in small groups, discuss some ways believers can guard against viewing our relationship with Christ as just something else on our schedules. Create on the board a list of the top five suggestions.

+ Write *priorities* on the board and call for volunteers to suggest how they determine their priorities each day.

+ Discuss how the biblical concept of slavery to Christ impacts the way we think about what is important in life.

+ Read Philippians 1:21. What does that verse teach about Paul's priorities? What lesson does Paul's example teach us?

React

+ While in small groups, instruct learners to identify their primary concerns upon arriving at church each week.
+ Next, instruct them to determine if their concerns are more self-centered or God-centered. Ask, "Are your primary concerns more about you or about God?"
+ Ask, "In light of what we've learned about being a slave, are your attitudes consistent with being God's slave? Why or why not?" Discuss responses.
+ Close with a time of prayer.

two

Ancient History, Timeless Truth

Read chapter 2 of *Slave* and complete the activities in chapter 2 of the Study Guide.

Rewind

+ Ask, "What do you consider to be the benefits of slavery for the slave?" Allow time for responses.
+ Ask, "Since God is our Master, what kind of experience should we expect as His slaves?" List responses on the board, calling attention to the evidence of God's gracious character that learners mention.

Rethink

+ Explain that slavery in the Roman world was as diverse as the number of masters who owned slaves. Whether slaves worked in the fields or in the city; whether they became farmers, household managers, or something else; whether or not they eventually gained their freedom; and whether the quality of their daily existence was positive or negative—everything rested in the master's hands. Each slave owner defined the nature of his slaves' lives. For their part, slaves had only one primary objective: to please the master in everything through their loyal obedience to him.

+ Remind learners that a slave's objective was to please his master in everything he did. Therefore, as slaves to God, we are to please Him in everything we do. Ask, "What are some areas of life that people often keep off-limits to God?" List responses on the board.

+ Remind learners that the exodus from Egypt did not give the Israelites complete autonomy, but a different kind of bondage. Those who had once been the property of Pharaoh became the Lord's possession.

+ Call for a volunteer to read aloud Exodus 19:1–8. Ask a few volunteers to discuss how they would have responded if they had been there at the foot of Mount Sinai.

+ Point out that many of the heroes of the faith are referred to as "slaves" in Scripture. Ask, "How does that fact affect your understanding of what it means to be a slave of God?"

+ Explain that being a slave is to be under the complete authority of someone else. It means rejecting personal autonomy and embracing the will of another. Ask, "Why is this concept so offensive to those who live in our society?" Call for responses.

Reflect

+ Remind learners that Paul, before his conversion, had arrogantly and hypocritically viewed himself as religiously superior to others. Ask, "What happened that allowed him to view himself as a slave?" Point out that Paul's salvation experience didn't change his personality; it changed his purpose, passions, and priorities.

- Call for three prearranged volunteers to share their conversion experiences. Then ask each volunteer, "How has God repurposed your passions?"
- Read aloud James 1:1. Remind learners that James could have referred to himself first as Jesus' brother. Rather, James chose to call himself a slave. Ask, "What does this say about his perspective on the Christian life?" Call for responses.
- Call for a volunteer to read aloud James 4:13–15. Discuss how this passage describes the attitude of genuine believers. Then ask, "How does your attitude toward life compare to that of James?" Call for responses.

React

- Call attention to the fact that our present and future relationships with God are set in the context of slavery. We are to be His slaves now, and we will be His slaves in heaven. Ask, "What should our response be to our God-given role as His slaves?" Discuss responses.
- Discuss what would happen to the vitality of our Christian lives if we embraced the idea of being slaves to Christ. List responses on the board.
- Ask, "Is the idea of being at God's mercy comforting or frightening to you? Why?" Call for responses.
- Remind learners that, for slaves, there is no area of life outside the boundaries of the master's control. Ask, "In what areas of life do you need to fully submit to God's control? What would happen if you did that?" Discuss responses.
- Close with a time of prayer.

three

The Good and Faithful Slave

Read chapter 3 of *Slave* and complete the activities in chapter 3 of the Study Guide.

Rewind

+ Arrange the class in small groups. Instruct some groups to discuss what it means to go from being a slave to sin to being a slave to Jesus Christ. Instruct other groups to talk about how their lives are different because of that transformation. After a few moments, call for reports from each group.
+ Ask, "If Jesus, our heavenly Master, were to evaluate your life right now, how pleased would He be with your attitude toward loving God and loving other people?" Call for responses.

Rethink

+ Explain that throughout the New Testament, believers are repeatedly called to embrace the perspective of those who belong to Christ and therefore lovingly submit to Him as Master. That kind of perspective has serious implications for how we, as believers, think and act.

+ Read aloud Romans 6:17–18 and then summarize the discussion of *Exclusive Ownership* on pages 44–45. Ask learners to respond in small groups to this question: "What is the difference between being a slave to Christ and being an employee of Christ?"

+ Call for a volunteer to read aloud 1 John 2:3. Point out that complete submission to Christ is evidence that we have come to know Him.

+ Remind learners that slaves had only one primary concern: to carry out the will of the master. In areas where they were given direct commands, they were required to obey. In areas where no direct command was given, they were to find ways to please the master as best they could. Tell learners to keep this in mind as you read a couple of verses from Colossians.

+ Read aloud Colossians 3:17, 23. Ask, "What elements of your life fall outside the boundaries of these verses?"

+ Read aloud Matthew 6:31–33 and list on the board some common things about which people worry.

+ Read aloud Philippians 4:6. Ask, "What should be your attitude in regard to the aspects of life mentioned above?" Call for responses.

Reflect

+ Read aloud Romans 14:12 and 2 Corinthians 5:10. Share with learners how these verses make you feel. Then call for volunteers to share their thoughts about these verses.

+ Say, "In serving our earthly masters, we also serve the Lord." Ask, "What should be a believer's attitude at work?" Discuss responses. Ask, "Why is it so hard to have a good attitude at work?"

+ Remind learners that according to the principle found in Colossians 4:1, Christian leaders should reflect godliness in their attitudes and actions toward those they lead. Discuss some things learners can do to better reflect Christ to those they lead. List key points on the board.

React

+ Ask, "What is the difference between living for earthly rewards and living for heavenly rewards?" List responses on the board.
+ Say, "It is easy to live for the praise and adoration of other people." Ask, "What happens to our spiritual fervor when we focus on being accepted by people?" Call for responses and discussion.
+ Explain that many believers resist the idea of accountability. They prefer a version of faith that suits their lifestyles and their interests. Many believers attend churches expecting to receive VIP treatment. Ask. "In light of biblical teaching, what would you say to someone who exhibited these attitudes and behaviors?" Call for responses.
+ Close with prayer.

four

The Lord and Master (Part 1)

Read chapter 4 of *Slave* and complete the activities in chapter 4 of the Study Guide.

Rewind

+ Begin the session by asking, "What traditions was John Huss trying to overturn? On what authority did he challenge those traditions?"
+ Continue the discussion by asking, "Why is it important for us to continually evaluate our traditions in light of God's Word? What should we do if our traditions don't measure up to the Scriptures?" Call for responses.

Rethink

+ Remind learners that when John Huss attempted to explain his writings, his voice was drowned out by the angry shouts of his accusers demanding that his books be burned. Though he appealed to reason, to his conscience, and even to the Word of God, his words went completely unheeded and ignored.
+ Arrange learners in small groups and assign one of the following questions to each group:

+ What happens in our world when believers speak up for the cause of Christ?
+ What are some evidences that our culture isn't interested in what the Bible has to say?
+ Who are some of the people to whom people regularly listen (from television, radio, or personal relationships)? What is their perspective on God? How does their perspective affect their advice?

After about 5 minutes, call for groups to report on their discussions.

+ Point out that John Huss argued against any mere man being the head of the church. Ask, "What can we do today to keep Jesus Christ as the focus of our worship?" Call for responses.
+ Ask, "Why is it sometimes easier to seek man's approval more than God's approval? Discuss responses.
+ Discuss some things believers can do to keep their focus more on pleasing God and less on pleasing themselves.

Reflect

+ Call for learners to identify some of the "authorities" that are popular in secular society. List responses on the board.
+ Remind learners that many "authorities" in our culture are popular rather than knowledgeable. Discuss some ways learners can discern between which authorities to accept and which to reject. Ask, "What is our final authority as believers?"
+ Share your plan for knowing and applying God's Word to your life. Then call for learners to share their strategies for knowing and applying God's Word to their lives.

React

- Call for learners to discuss some ways we can keep our love for Christ our top priority. Point out that there is a difference between loving Christ and participating in religious activities.
- Ask, "How should we, as Christians, respond when we are ridiculed or rejected by unbelievers?"
- Call for volunteers to share stories about people they know who are steadfast in their faith and unwilling to compromise in any area of life.
- Ask, "If threatened with arrest for your belief in God, what would be your response?" Discuss responses.
- Close with prayer.

five

The Lord and Master (Part 2)

Read chapter 5 of *Slave* and complete the activities in chapter 5 of the Study Guide.

Rewind

+ Call for volunteers to discuss some ways they have seen the gospel of Christ distorted. Be careful not to encourage the criticism of individuals—only distorted viewpoints.
+ Arrange learners in small groups and instruct them to develop a strategy believers can use to protect themselves against distorted versions of the gospel. Call for groups to report their strategies.
+ Discuss some of the dangers of believing in a distorted version of the gospel. Encourage learners to take advantage of the opportunities they have to study God's Word and to participate in discipleship classes.

Rethink

+ Remind learners that many leaders of the contemporary evangelical movement have lost interest in doctrine. The current of mainstream evangelicalism is driven by pragmatic concerns, not theological ones. Church growth gurus worry about what draws a crowd, not about what the Bible says. Because it successfully appeals to unredeemed flesh, prosperity preachers make *man* the master, as if Christ were some sort of genie in a bottle—obliged to grant health, wealth, and happiness to those who send enough money. Even within some conservative circles, pragmatic worldly methods (including crass humor and coarse speech) and almost boundless adaptations of the worst of worldly music are aggressively defended as long as they get visible results. The sad reality is that popularity, not faithfulness to Christ and His Word, has become evangelicalism's new standard of measure and its current brand of no-lordship ideology.

+ Ask, "When you attend church, are you more interested in a good show or in hearing God's truth even if it steps on your toes?" Discuss responses.

+ Cite some examples of the messages we hear on television, radio, and on the Internet that contradict biblical teaching. Discuss some steps to determining if something is true or false.

+ Call for volunteers to read aloud 1 Corinthians 7:23 and Romans 6:17–18. Call for learners to summarize each passage.

+ Read aloud Romans 14:7–8. Ask, "What does this passage say about the role of the Master in the life of a believer?" Call for responses.

Reflect

+ Read aloud Philippians 1:21. Ask, "How would you explain Paul's perspective on life? Why could he say that dying is gain?"

+ Remind learners that believers are often tempted to compromise, disobey, and draw back from their initial commitment to Christ. Ask, "How can we maintain a fervent focus on the Lord?" List responses on the board.

+ Continue the discussion by reading aloud 1 John 1:9 and asking, "What should we do when we fail to obey Him?"
+ Read aloud Mark 12:30 and call for volunteers to share their personal insights into this verse.

React

+ Invite a volunteer to read aloud Colossians 3:17, 23. Ask, "How can we make obedience to these instructions a reality in our lives?" Discuss responses.
+ Call for volunteers to share some of the ways that God has allowed them to use their abilities and gifts in His service.
+ Write on the board *Jesus is the Master, and we are slaves.* Ask, "How does this truth affect your daily life?" Call for responses.
+ Close with prayer.

six

Our Lord and Our God

Read chapter 6 of *Slave* and complete the activities in chapter 6 of the Study Guide.

Rewind

+ Write the following sentence on the board: *We have a duty to obey and worship God.* As learners arrive, call attention to the sentence you have written. After everyone is seated, read aloud Romans 12:1–2. Ask, "What is the relationship between our worship and our obedience?" Call for responses.
+ Ask, "What verses and biblical truths underscore the deity of Jesus Christ?" List responses on the board.

Rethink

+ Remind learners that as believers who confess the lordship of Christ, they are duty bound to obey Him in everything. As slaves to righteousness, they are "under obligation" (Rom. 8:12; cf. 6:18) to honor God in how they live. Yet, because they belong to Christ, their motivation to obey is far more profound than mere duty. Read John 14:15, 23.

+ Remind learners that slaves are required to obey Christ in everything. Ask, "Why is this such as hard thing for many believers to do?" Call for responses.
+ Continue the discussion by asking, "What is the proper motivation for our obedience to Him?"
+ Read John 14:15. Ask, "Is it possible to love Jesus and not obey Him?" Discuss responses.
+ Explain that the only right response to Christ's lordship is wholehearted submission, loving obedience, and passionate worship. Ask, "Why is each of these a proper response to Christ's authority?" Call for responses.
+ Read aloud Luke 6:46. Ask, "What would you say if Jesus asked you this question?" Call for responses.

Reflect

+ Call for a volunteer to read aloud James 2:17 and 1 John 2:4–5.
+ Ask, "If actions speak louder than words, what is the lifestyle of the average believer saying about his or her love for God?" Discuss responses.
+ Arrange learners in pairs or small groups and encourage them to discuss this question: "What do you need to change in your life so that your actions match what you claim to believe?" Call for volunteers to share highlights of their discussions.

React

+ Remind learners that the life of a slave results in the ultimate experience of peace and joy. Read aloud Philippians 4:6. Ask, "If your peace and joy are indicators of your level of confidence in God, how well are you doing at trusting Him in all things?" Call for responses.

+ Returning to pairs or small groups, ask, "What decisions or challenges are you facing? How can you trust God to see you through those situations?" Encourage each group to spend a few moments in prayer for one another.

+ Remind learners that the greatest glory for a slave is the realization that he is honoring His master. As you pray, ask God to give you the passion for serving Him with joy and sharing Him with confidence.

+ Close with prayer.

seven

The Slave Market of Sin

R ead chapter 7 of *Slave* and complete the activities in chapter 7 of the Study Guide.

Rewind

+ As learners arrive, assign them to pairs or small groups and instruct them to discuss the following questions (written on the board):
+ In what ways does the uniqueness of your testimony help you realize what it means to be a slave to sin?
+ As a believer in Jesus Christ, how does it make you feel to recognize that you have been set free from sin?
+ After 5–7 minutes, call for volunteers to share summaries of their discussions.

Rethink

+ Remind learners that John Newton repeatedly contrasted bondage to sin with the redemption he received through Jesus Christ. He portrayed himself in his lost condition as a slave who, if Christ had not rescued him, would have remained in captivity. Point out that

Newton's hymns resound with the glorious theme of deliverance from his own wickedness. Newton remembered what it was like to be unconverted, to be one of those who was under complete control of Satan.

+ Encourage learners to compare their bondage to sin to the redemption they received at salvation. Ask, "How can you describe the difference between these two states of existence?" Call for responses.

+ Ask, "If your life were declared in a hymn, what would be its theme?" List responses on the board.

+ Continue the discussion by asking, "Why has John Newton's hymn 'Amazing Grace' resounded with so many people?"

+ Point out that we are never free; our lives are under the control of something or someone. As unbelievers, we lived under the power of sin. But now we are under the power of God. Ask, "What differences have you seen in your life as a result of that radical change?" Call for volunteers to respond.

+ Read aloud Romans 8:1. Ask, "How does it make you feel to understand that we have not only been set free from sin's oppression but also from its deadly consequences?" Call for responses.

Reflect

+ Ask, "If submission to God's will is pure joy, then why do so many believers resist obeying God's will for their lives?" Discuss responses.

+ List on the board responses to this question, "What are some of the ethical implications of your freedom in Christ?" Add others ideas from your personal preparation.

+ Read aloud Ephesians 5:3–10. Ask learners to discuss how believers should respond to those who, under the guise of friendship, will have a negative influence on them.

+ Guide learners to create a list of ways to guard their moral purity in a world that seems to have no moral standards. List steps on the board.
+ Call for volunteers to identify some things they have eliminated from their lives in order to protect themselves from immoral and unethical influences. List responses on the board.

React

+ Ask, "In what way is Israel's physical liberation from Egypt a picture of the spiritual liberation that sinners experience when they are set free from sin?"
+ Ask, "Do you agree that sin is a harsh taskmaster? Why or why not?" Discuss responses.
+ Remind learners that, once rescued from slavery, the Israelites returned to the bondage of disobedience. Ask, "How does your knowledge of God's Word protect you from the bondage of disobedience?" Call for volunteers to share responses.
+ Close with prayer.

eight

Bound, Blind, and Dead

Read chapter 8 of *Slave* and complete the activities in chapter 8 of the Study Guide.

Rewind

- Read aloud 1 Peter 2:18–19. Ask, "In New Testament times, how would a harsh master have served as a fitting illustration of the oppression that characterizes sin?" Call for responses.
- Continue the discussion by asking, "How has your life changed since being freed from slavery to sin?" Call on several volunteers to respond.
- Ask, "How is slavery to God different from slavery to sin?" Write responses on the board.

Rethink

- Remind learners that sin corrupts the entire person—infecting the soul, polluting the mind, defiling the conscience, contaminating the affections, and poisoning the will. It is the life-destroying, soul-condemning cancer that festers and grows in every unredeemed human heart like an incurable gangrene.

+ Note that our society has a tendency to minimize sin and its effects. Ask, "How does God's Word describe the seriousness of sin?"
+ Read John 8:31–36. Ask, "What is the sinner's only hope of freedom from sin?"
+ Continue the discussion by asking, "How does Jesus define true freedom in this passage?" Discuss the responses.
+ Say, "Scripture is clear: unless the Spirit of God gives spiritual life, all sinners are completely unable to change their fallen nature or to rescue themselves from sin and divine judgment. They can neither initiate nor accomplish any aspect of their redemption" (p. 122).
+ Read aloud Ephesians 2:1–10. Ask, "Do you agree with this passage? Why or why not?" Discuss responses.
+ Explain that pride makes us think we are not as sinful as we really are. We rationalize our sin by focusing on the more significant sin of others. Read aloud Luke 18:10–14. Ask, "What is God's response to prideful, self-righteous people?"

Reflect

+ Point out that the people to whom Jesus spoke were involved in religious activity, yet they hypocritically clung to sin in their hearts. What they claimed to believe contradicted the way that they lived. Ask, "What is the relationship between what you claim to believe and the way you live?" Call for responses.
+ Read aloud Romans 3:10–12. Ask, "In light of Paul's words, how can you and I stand blameless before God?" Call for responses.
+ Call for learners to discuss among themselves this question: "If someone claims to be a believer yet continues to live like a slave to sin, what is that person's true attitude toward God's grace?" After a few moments, call for volunteers to report their conclusions.

+ While in small, single-gender groups, learners should discuss some ways through which temptation to sin enters their lives. Be careful to protect the privacy of learners as they share. Refrain from putting anyone on the spot to respond to this activity.
+ Ask, "What is a biblical strategy for resisting temptation? What is the role of accountability groups in protecting ourselves from sin?" Discuss responses.

React

+ Call for learners to share the initials only of some people they know who seem to flaunt being slaves to sin. List initials on the board.
+ Ask, "What should be our roles in the lives of the people we've listed here?" Discuss responses.
+ Ask, "In what specific ways can you pray for these people? Only the truth of the gospel can set them free from their sin. Will you commit yourself to sharing the good news of salvation with these people?"
+ Close with prayer.

nine

Saved from Sin, Slaved by Grace

R ead chapter 9 of *Slave* and complete the activities in chapter 9 of the Study Guide.

Rewind

+ Write the following question on the board, "How does it make you feel knowing that God chose you?" As learners arrive, encourage them to discuss their responses to this question. As the session begins, call for volunteers to share their responses.
+ Ask, "If God predestined us to be freed from slavery to sin, why do so many professing Christians remain entangled in sinful lifestyles?" Discuss responses.
+ Continue the discussion by reading aloud 1 John 2:4–5. Ask, "How valid is a profession of faith that does not result in a transformed life?"

Rethink

God's will in salvation is singular, dependent on nothing other than His uninfluenced, free, electing choice. Therefore, the Holy Spirit works where

He wills, the Son gives life to whomever He wishes, and unless the Father draws them, unbelievers cannot come to Christ.

+ Arrange learners in three groups and assign one of the passages below to each group. Instruct groups to read the passage and to identify its main point. After a few moments, call for groups to report their findings.

> John 8:36
> 2 Corinthians 4:6
> Ephesians 2:4–5

+ Explain that God's sovereign grace includes not only the gift of salvation but also the repentant faith necessary for receiving that gift. Ask, "In light of that, how much of our salvation can we take credit for? What should our response be to God for initiating and accomplishing everything in our salvation?"
+ Call for a volunteer to read aloud 2 Thessalonians 2:13–14. Discuss what this passage has to say about a believer's purpose in life.
+ Call for learners to suggest some ways a believer can help nonbelieving friends understand the magnitude of God's love for them.

Reflect

+ Read aloud Romans 8:1–2. Call attention to the two laws that are at work in our lives. Discuss some of the evidences of each law and encourage learners to reflect on which law is controlling their lives.
+ Explain that God's gift of redemption brings salvation from both sin's oppression and sin's consequences—and one day from its very

existence. Though we are freed from the eternal consequences of sin, we are subject to the earthly consequences of our sin. Encourage learners to think about common temptations that Christians face. Ask, "What are some of the earthly consequences that come when Christians give in to those temptations?" Call for learners to share their thoughts.

+ Continue the discussion by asking, "In what way is the fear of such consequences a deterrent to sin?"

+ Ask learners to consider the message their lifestyle sends to God about His grace. Ask, "Based on your lifestyle, are you enslaved to Christ or sin?" Call for discussion.

· Read aloud Romans 6:23. Ask, "According to that verse, what are the wages of sin?" (The answer is *eternal death*.)

+ Then ask, "What is the free gift of faith in Christ?" (The answer is *eternal life*.)

+ Write *death* and *life* on the board. Ask, "Which offers the better reward? Why?" Call for responses.

React

+ Remind learners that the freed in Christ are not aimless or purposeless. They have been freed from sin in order that they may give themselves wholly to serving God. Ask, "How are you serving God with your time, energy, talents, and money?" Call for responses. Be prepared to offer a list of volunteer opportunities available in your church.

+ Allow a few moments for learners to identify some activities in which they are presently involved that will need to be adjusted or eliminated.

+ State that our freedom in Christ does not give us the right to decide what is right or wrong. We are obligated to pursue righteousness and right living. Ask, "What are some moral boundaries (derived from the Bible) that you need to establish or reinforce in your own life?"

+ Close with prayer.

ten

From Slaves to Sons (Part 1)

Read chapter 10 of *Slave* and complete the activities in chapter 10 of the Study Guide.

Rewind

+ Call for three prearranged volunteers to share their testimonies by talking about how they were not only freed from sin and made slaves to righteousness but were also adopted into the family of God.
+ Arrange learners in pairs or small groups and remind them that our salvation experience puts the old man to death and brings new life. Instruct them to discuss these questions: "Would your friends say you exhibit more evidence of the old man or the new life? Why?" After a few moments, call the class back together and call for volunteers to share their discussions.

Rethink

+ Remind learners that having delivered us from the destitution of sin, God has not only received us as His slaves—but He has also welcomed us into His household and made us members of His very family. He not only rescued us, purchased us, befriended us, and took us in; He has also adopted us, thereby transforming those who were formerly children of wrath into the sons and daughters of righteousness.

+ To further explore this topic, arrange learners in pairs or small groups and instruct them to consider the following questions:

> + What does it mean to be a child of God?
> + We have been adopted into God's family. Why is human adoption such a powerful metaphor of this spiritual reality?
> + What thoughts come to mind as you consider God's love toward us?

+ Read aloud Romans 8:14–17. Call for volunteers to share their paraphrases of these verses.
+ Point out that as the adopted children of God, we can rest assured in knowing that we have been given a permanent place in the family of God. Call for volunteers to talk about their attitudes toward God in response to this biblical truth.
+ Read aloud Ephesians 5:8 and Hebrews 12:7. Ask, "In light of the fact that we are God's children and He is our Father, how should we conduct ourselves in this world?" Call for responses.

Reflect

+ Call for a volunteer to read aloud Romans 8:28. Talk about what this verse says and what it does not say.
+ Read aloud Galatians 4:4–7. Call for volunteers to suggest ideas for how to explain this passage to someone who doesn't understand what it means to be a follower of Christ.
+ Arrange learners in small groups and instruct them to read Romans

8, listing three to four main points Paul made in this passage. After a few moments, call for groups to report. List responses on the board.

+ Review the responses above, talking about how each point affects the way we view our relationship with God.

React

+ Ask, "In what ways can you better reflect God's unconditional love toward the people you encounter each day?" List responses on the board.
+ Say, "If God is our Master, then He is our Father; if He is our Father, then He is our Master." Ask for volunteers to explain how those two realities fit together.
+ Read aloud Matthew 6:31–34. Remind learners that, as a child of God, you can trust your heavenly Father for your needs. Arrange learners in pairs or small groups and encourage them to discuss the needs they are trusting God to meet in their lives. Point out the difference between needs and wants.
+ Close with prayer.

eleven

From Slaves to Sons (Part 2)

Read chapter 11 of *Slave* and complete the activities in chapter 11 of the Study Guide.

Rewind

+ On the board, write *eternal judgment* and draw an arrow toward this phrase written to the right: *child of the King*. As learners arrive, challenge them to write down how they feel knowing that they have moved from one state to the other.
+ Read aloud 2 Corinthians 6:17–18, calling attention to what it says about our relationship with God.
+ Read aloud the very next verse, 2 Corinthians 7:1. Ask, "What are the implications of our relationship with God?"

Rethink

Revisit the story of Mephibosheth. What a magnificent picture of our spiritual adoption by God. We were not seeking Him, yet He found us and saved us, just as David did for Mephibosheth. We were God's enemies, yet He made us His friends. We could offer Him nothing in return, yet He bestowed on us an inheritance we did not deserve. All of this is ours by grace through faith in His only begotten Son, Jesus Christ.

+ Point out that as adopted slaves, our names are written in the Book of Life, from which they can never be erased. Ask. "What inheritance is yours because of your status as God's child?" List responses on the board.
+ Read aloud 2 Corinthians 4:17–18. Call for volunteers to discuss some ways the reality of their future inheritance affects their perspective on this life.
+ Call for a volunteer to read aloud Romans 8:15. Review the verse, identifying Paul's message to his readers. Ask why the message was so important then, and why it is so important now.
+ Read aloud Ephesians 1:3–6. Call for volunteers to identify some of the spiritual blessings that God has given to believers through Jesus Christ. Ask, "How are those blessings used in service to God in your daily life?" Call for responses.
+ Read aloud Psalm 16:5. Explain that David viewed everything in light of His relationship with God. Ask. "Do you view all of life from a God-centered perspective, or do you view God from a world-centered perspective?" Discuss responses.

Talk about the differences between these two perspectives.

Reflect

+ Look again at Romans 8:15. Ask, "Why do we no longer need to be afraid?"
+ Continue the discussion by reading aloud 1 John 4:17–18.
+ Read aloud Romans 8:29–31. Discuss God's promise to those He justifies and what the promise means for us today.

+ Call for a volunteer to read aloud 1 John 2:19. Explain that a true believer can never lose his salvation. Once adopted into God's family, he becomes a child of God forever. Ask, "According to this verse, what is the spiritual condition of one who claims to know Christ but later falls away?" (Answer: He was never saved.)
+ Read aloud John 6:39–40 and John 10:28–29. Point out that Jesus said that one who belongs to Him can never be taken away. Ask learners to reflect on the significance of this fact.

React

+ Arrange learners in pairs or small groups and assign each one of the following passages. Instruct them to identify what their passage says about our position as believers in Christ.

  Romans 8:1
  1 Peter 1:5
  Philippians 1:6
  1 Thessalonians 5:23–24
  2 Thessalonians 3:3
  Jude 24–25

+ After a few moments, call for group members to read aloud the passage and then share their findings.
+ Read aloud Romans 6:1. Ask, "Since we are forgiven, why is it important that believers refrain from sinning?" Call for discussion.
+ Point out that continuing in a lifestyle of sin after "salvation" is evidence that the person never really experienced salvation in the first place. Ask, "How do those who know you best know that your salvation is real?" Allow time for reflection and reaction.
+ Remind learners that as God's children, we no longer should fear

death, because it will usher us into the presence of our heavenly Father. Ask, "How has your attitude toward death changed since you accepted Jesus as your Lord and Savior?" Call for responses.

+ Close with prayer.

twelve

Ready to Meet the Master

Read chapter 12 of *Slave* and complete the activities in chapter 12 of the Study Guide.

Rewind

+ Write the following question on the board: "If called upon today to give an account of your stewardship of the resources, abilities, blessings, and opportunities entrusted to you, what would you say to God?" As learners arrive, encourage them to reflect on this question.
+ Ask, "What would be God's reaction to your stewardship of the blessings He has entrusted to you?" Call for responses.
+ Arrange learners in pairs or small groups. Encourage them to discuss any God-given resources that they have mismanaged. Then instruct them to identify some ways they can start investing the resources God has given them for His purposes. Call for groups to report their discussions.

Rethink

+ Share the following with the learners: Though we do not know when the Master will return, we do know one thing for certain: *one day He will come back* (Mark 13:33–37). That simple fact should motivate us to greater holiness and service. It should also comfort and enthuse us, if we are living obediently. A slave only fears the master's return if he has been unfaithful. But for Christ's slaves who have worked hard and served well, the Master's arrival is a moment of great celebration. For them, His coming represents entrance into His joy and the beginning of great reward.

+ Read aloud Philippians 2:10–11. Explain that every person will make the declaration described in this passage. Ask, "What is the difference between those who make the declaration while they are alive and those who make it at judgment?" (Those who make it before death receive eternal life. Those who only make it after death receive eternal separation from God in a real place called hell.)

+ Reproduce on the board the line below. Talk about the obedient slave having nothing to fear in the Master's return. Point out that believers should be obedient and unafraid.

disobedient/afraid ←—————————————→ obedient/unafraid

+ Remind learners that believers who spend their lives in temporal and worthless pursuits should expect minimal reward from Christ. Ask, "Based on your spiritual investment, what degree of reward can you expect from God?" Call for responses.

+ Read aloud Ephesians 6:5–9. Call for volunteers to suggest how they would answer a new believer's question about how he or she should live. Point out that it is hypocritical to offer advice that we are not exhibiting in our lives.

+ Share with learners that, though he would often be rejected and persecuted, Paul was far more concerned with obeying his divine calling than with gaining man's approval. Only one thing mattered— pleasing the Master. Ask learners to identify some of the primary concerns they see in people's lives today. List responses on the board.

Reflect

+ Write *success* on the board. Ask, "What are some standards by which people measure success?" List responses on the board. Point out that many believers measure success in worldly terms.
+ Continue the discussion by asking, "What is God's standard of success?"
+ Ask, "If you achieve the American Dream, what will be God's reaction?" Call for responses.
+ Continue the discussion by reading aloud Mark 8:36. Ask, "How important is worldly wealth when compared to eternity?"
+ Write *citizens* on the board and ask, "How can believers live on earth as citizens of heaven?" Call for responses.
+ Explain that citizenship provides certain privileges. Discuss some of the privileges of citizenship in heaven. List them on the board. Then say, "Citizenship also brings certain responsibilities." Discuss some of the responsibilities citizens of heaven have. List them on the board.
+ Refer to the list of responsibilities and ask, "How effectively are you carrying out your responsibilities? What excuses are you making for not doing what God has called you to do?" Remind learners that we are not saved by what we do; but because we are saved, we are called to live in obedience to God's expectations.

React

+ Ask, "What does it mean to 'walk in a manner worthy of the God who calls you into His own kingdom and glory'? (1 Thess. 2:12)? Call for responses.
+ Explain that our lives are synonymous with our citizenship. Our priorities, passions, and pursuits have all been changed because our very identity has been transformed. Call for volunteers to identify

some of the ways their priorities, passions, and pursuits have been changed as a result of their relationship with Christ.

+ Read aloud Revelation 22:3–5. Ask, "What should be the effect of this passage on your attitude toward life?" Call for responses.
+ Close with prayer.

thirteen

The Riches of the Paradox

R ead chapter 13 of *Slave* and complete the activities in Chapter 13 of the Study Guide.

Rewind

As learners arrive, direct them to small groups in which they will discuss the following questions. After a few moments, call for groups to report summaries of their discussions.

+ Where should we go to learn God's will?
+ Would you say that you are living to please yourself or living to please God? What is the difference between these two philosophies?
+ What does it mean to be a slave of Christ? How is that different from merely being His servant?

Rethink

As Christians, *we are slaves of Christ*. What a radical difference that truth should make in our daily lives! We no longer live for ourselves. Rather, we make it our aim to please the Master in everything. After reminding learners of this truth, complete the following activities.

• Write the four paradoxes below on the board. Guide learners through a discussion of the questions and Scripture passages below, drawing on the earlier lessons for supporting information.

1. *Slavery brings freedom.* True freedom can only be found through slavery to Christ.

   • Ask, "Why is this truth so hard for modern believers to accept?" Call for responses.
   • Read aloud Romans 6:16–18. Discuss Paul's thoughts about this issue.

2. *Slavery ends prejudice.* Slavery to Christ is the path to reconciliation and unity within the body of Christ. When believers realize that they are all *slaves*, called to model the humility of the ultimate slave, it becomes obvious how they ought to treat others.

   • Read aloud Philippians 2:5–7. Ask, "If our attitude should be the same as Christ's, how should we treat other people?" Call for responses.

3. *Slavery magnifies grace.* Our slavery to Christ magnifies the wonder of His infinite grace. It is important to understand that our service to Him is also an undeserved gift—one we both receive and accomplish by His grace. Our ability to serve Him is only possible because He enables us to do so "by the strength which God supplies; so that in all things God might be glorified through Jesus Christ" (1 Peter 4:11).

   • Read aloud Matthew 6:24. Ask, "What are some of the 'masters' that deter people from submitting to the one, true Master?" Call for discussion.

+ Read aloud 1 Corinthians 15:10. Point out Paul's attitude toward serving God. Ask, "What is your attitude toward serving God?" Allow time for responses.

4. *Slavery pictures salvation.* God has expressed the riches of our salvation using the symbolism of slavery. In eternity past, God chose those whom He would save. In our own lifetime, He rescued us from slavery to sin and delivered us into the kingdom of His dear Son. Christ's atoning work on the cross redeemed us, such that we were purchased by Him; and having been bought with a price, we are now His possession. We have been liberated from sin, and now as slaves to righteousness, we possess a glorious freedom that will be ours for all of eternity future.

+ Read aloud Titus 2:11–14. Call for learners to rephrase those verses in their own words.
+ State that salvation is by faith alone (Titus 3:5–7). Yet remind learners that genuine saving faith is never alone. It inevitably produces "fruit in keeping with repentance" (Matt. 3:8), thereby evidencing a transformed heart. Ask, "In what ways has your life been transformed?" Call for responses.

Reflect

+ Ask, "What does it mean to be a Christian?" Call for responses.

React

+ Say, "Now let me rephrase that question. How has your study of slavery to Christ impacted your understanding of the Christian life?" Call for responses.

+ Continue the discussion by asking, "What are the implications of that concept in your daily walk with God?"
+ As time allows, ask, "What are your closing thoughts in regard to your status as God's slave?"
+ Close with prayer.